The secret mind of addiction.

A new perspective for life.

Copyright © 2025 by Robert De Pinto. All rights reserved.

No part of this publication may be reproduced, distributed, or transmitted in any form or by any means, including photocopying, recording, or other electronic or mechanical methods, without the prior written permission of the author, except in the case of brief quotations embodied in critical reviews and certain other non-commercial uses permitted by copyright law.

For permission requests, send an email to contact@lifebeyondthinking.com

First Edition Published by:
Global Wellness Media
Stratedgy LLC
440 N Barranca Ave #2027
Covina, California, 91723
(866) 467-9090
GlobalWellnessMedia.com

Publisher's Note: The views expressed in this work are solely those of the authors and do not necessarily reflect the views of the publisher, and the publisher hereby disclaims any responsibilities for them.

Editor: Janna Hockenjos

Illustrations: Robert De Pinto

The secret mind of addiction / Robert De Pinto.
ISBN: 978-1-957343-29-7 (Paperback)
ISBN: 978-1-957343-30-3 (e-book)

Safety and Self-care

Keeping yourself (and others) safe is the first and most important part of any work or activity in life.

If at any point you feel unsafe reading this book or following its suggestions, please pause, and take care of yourself (and others).

Everything in this book and the larger body of work (called Life Beyond Thinking®) is suggestive only.

You are responsible for your own actions, self-care, and the care of those around you.

Acknowledgements

Thank you to all the people that have supported me and this work over the years.

And to the unwavering love and support of my family. Thank you.

To everyone that said no. Sometimes it wasn't a fit, sometimes lessons for me. It all helped clear the way. It is appreciated.

To my publisher Eric D. Groleau, for your support for this book, and of me, thank you. It would not be here without you.

Thank you to my editor Janna Hockenjos. Your patience, insight and straight talking has been invaluable on so many levels. A journey I am deeply grateful for.

To God, for every single thing, thank you.

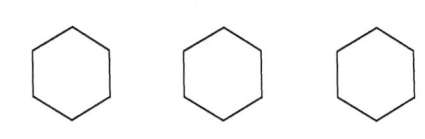

Human Powered

No AI was used in the writing, editing or production of this book.

100% human.

○ ○ ○

Contents

1. Introduction — 1
2. Suggestions When Reading — 5
3. Addiction or Purpose — 7
4. The Many Forms of Addiction — 11
5. A New Perspective — 15
6. How Addiction Escalates — 27
7. The Clues to Getting Free — 35
8. The Way Forward — 43
9. What Helped and Hurt — 57
11. In Conclusion — 71
12. FREE Resources — 73
13. Author Bio — 75
14. LBT Books and Programs — 77
15. W.H. Murray Quote — 79

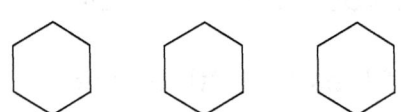

Introduction

I now believe life is simple. We just got the wrong map and the wrong rules.

Looking back, I really only wanted two things:
- the nightmare to end,
- and to know exactly what, why, and how, so I could get on and live my life fully, without the palaver, without the fear, and without the unearned shame and guilt (they are killers).

In short, I wanted to be free.

What made the journey more challenging was that while I was doing some things very right, I was also doing some things very wrong. Then mix in unresolved trauma, an epic failure, and a society filling up on lies and gaslighting, and the confusion grew too much to discern what was what, and getting well became a different trap.

This book aims to cut through the noise. To sharpen your focus with one simple and clear perspective on the root cause of addiction, so that you can have a faster and more direct path to freedom.

So, if you are tired of disempowerment, mixed messages, and feeling limited by existing programs or your own efforts, and if you want a new understanding of what's really going on in your mind and your life, read on.

– Introduction –

Most of the programs, coaches, books, treatments, and therapies I have experienced seemed well-intentioned. Some helped, some didn't, and some I now believe kept me trapped as a slave to suffering. I was better and not dead, but I certainly wasn't living fully or deeply at peace. And I certainly didn't have a clear, consistent answer to what, why, or how to get free forever.

My desire for a unified answer led to the development of **Life Beyond Thinking®**, and the book you are reading now, contains elements from that larger body of work.

The secret mind of addiction shares a novel concept, illustrating that the root cause and the solution to many of our addictions (and subsequent problems) starts in the mind, growing from a specific set of thoughts which then impacts our response to life. And because we don't have the full map or the right rules, we remain hurt, stuck, tired, and lost.

The model you will discover in the pages ahead has been through years of experimentation and hundreds of use cases, and still holds true. I believe *The secret mind of addiction* is that right map.

As you read on, please note that sun, nature, nutrition, exercise, sleep, and an in-person community of quality people help in any transformation work, as it does in regular everyday living. Though in my experience, these aspects of life alone, do not solve the root cause, nor adequately answer the what, why, and how of life, which as you will see, is inextricably linked to addiction.

Do not forget that chemical addiction in the body is real, and detox can be life threatening. Please seek medical care if that is you.

In the last chapter, "What Helped and Hurt," I explore and challenge popular themes from recovery, spirituality, and wellness, with the aim to further sharpen your perspective and accelerate your path to freedom.

At the end, I provide links to FREE Resources that offer additional tools, insights, and the opportunity for Q&A on the topics in this book.

Irrespective of whether you are in active addiction or recovery, the insights contained in *The secret mind of addiction,* should help clear the noise to illuminate the path to true freedom.

Onward,
Robert De Pinto

Suggestions When Reading

A few suggestions to help you get the most from this book.

Throughout the text, I am going to use very simple diagrams. They might seem too basic, even trivial and comical, but do not dismiss them. They are a powerful tool to objectively look at your mind and life. They are the foundation of what, why, and how, and they are immutable.

This is you... :)

When reading, please look at the diagrams beside the text. Take a breath to reflect and observe your own thoughts and life. They will help you view yourself, without being stuck in the middle of a thought storm filled with prejudgement.

I reference various addictions throughout the text, but I am not playing favorites, you can interchange almost any addiction for the ones I mention, and the model still holds true.

Addiction
or Purpose

There are two major connotations of addiction. The negative and the positive (pre-1900s).

The negative is the obvious. The repeated behaviors that ultimately cause consequences that you consciously do not want. Whether it's visible to the world or kept hidden, you know it's there.

The positive is being consumed by an idea, project, or calling. Something you can't put down because it "captured your imagination" and you must pursue it. Others might say you're harming yourself, but it gives you life.

As a child, I was inspired by the positive. Both the people and what they achieved. They chased their dreams and burned the ships at the shore to do it. Off on an adventure. Everything was possible. Single-minded persistence seemed to be "The way."

Today, there are sections of society that imply this is bad. We need to calm down, fit in, reduce ambition, blindly do what "they" say. Don't stand out. Don't try too hard or dream too big. Mediocrity works. Individuality and aspiration are a faulty ego. All are lies to imprison us, and subsequently they all connect us to the negative addictive pattern.

Let's quickly scan a few accepted models of addiction for added context.

> "Addiction is the presence of the **4 C's**:
> - **C**raving
> - loss of **C**ontrol of amount or frequency of use
> - **C**ompulsion to use
> - use despite **C**onsequences."
>
> The Centre for Addiction and Mental Health, Canada

> "The Syndrome Model suggests that people inherit, encounter, and accumulate different life influences and experiences, which can interact or accumulate to form factors, ranging from neurobiological to psychosocial. Some factors or combinations of factors can increase the likelihood of addiction. If people then gain access to an object of addiction, they might develop increased motivation to seek and use the object (e.g., alcohol, drugs, gambling). Within the Syndrome Model, the emphasis is on the relationship between the person and their object of addiction. Addiction resides in the relationship and not in the object."
>
> Cambridge Health Alliance,
> Division on addiction.

> "Addiction is defined as a chronic, relapsing disorder characterized by compulsive drug seeking and use despite adverse consequences. It is considered a brain disorder, because it involves functional changes to brain circuits involved in reward, stress, and self-control. Those changes may last a long time after a person has stopped taking drugs."
>
> The National Institute on Drug Abuse, USA

There are two sides to these definitions. First, there is the objective negative. Physical decay, and destruction of life, for the addicts and people around them. This side is clear and hard to dispute. Second, is the subjective which can falsely restrict us and cause more confusion. When we have subjective third parties telling us what normal is, what adverse consequences are, and to do what they say to fit into their definition of "good" or "normal," my questions are: Who are they to decide? And who decided who decides? And why?

Fitting in, being normal, doing what "they say" in sobriety is in one sense essential, but for me, there were contradictions. I did not feel fully alive. My inner compass called for something more. An indisputable, objective map, and not just another person telling me to "fit in."

The Many Forms of Addiction

I want to zoom out to broaden our perspective and perception of addictions. Let's list the obvious, and consider the less obvious:

- phones, tablets, social media, gaming
- alcohol, narcotics, tobacco, vapes
- weed, pot, cannabis
- porn, sex, gambling
- shopping, online shopping
- food, highly processed foods
- treats (marketed as good things)
- physical self-harm
- lying to self, lying to others
- corruption, hypocrisy
- power, control over others
- cheating, stealing
- political ideology derangements
- endless drama, arguments, chaos
- getting well forever
- wellness rituals, guided visualizations
- journaling, meditation, gratitude lists*
- sacred plant medicine
- procrastination
- sugar dating (e.g., free dinners, gold digging)
- whining, complaining, excuses, gossip
- codependence
- being of service to everyone but yourself
- narcissistic abuse

* Gratitude is essential, but can be misdirected. See the FREE Resources section for more.

- under earning
- debt, usury
- self-loathing, worthlessness
- victimhood, helplessness
- group meetings
- virtue signaling
- AI, op-ed, mainstream media
- fantasy, nostalgia, hoarding
- sport as avoidance
- failure, self-sabotage
- a life you hate but keep coming back to
- suffering itself

This list is not exhaustive, but you get the idea. (Perhaps circle the ones that you can relate to.)

Some of these may not present as addictions. In fact, some will even appear very helpful. In the short term they are. However, what they do is manage symptoms, and in time, that management can become a way to retreat from life and from living. Management of symptoms avoids the root cause and becomes an escape from what we are meant to be doing now or from our deepest calling and greatest contribution to life.

Negative addictions are an adverse response to life, as is the prolonged management of symptoms.

If we are to get free from both, we require unwavering and complete honesty with self. And for that, we need to see what's going on in our mind (thoughts, words, and actions) with respect to life.

We need a new perspective.

A New Perspective

To fully understand addiction, the drinking, drugs, food, porn, compulsive shopping, etc. (and mental health in general) we must look at the progression of our life, and the context of the world in which we live.

We need to zoom out past our family and friends, past society as a whole, and get beyond politics, religion or geography. Eventually we want to zoom out so far that we can observe consciousness itself. From that perspective, we can see how our thoughts, words, and actions, all fit together in an objective and cohesive way. We can better see the patterns, and the root cause.

The root cause of addiction ends up being very simple—it all starts with one thought in our mind, and progresses from there.

— A NEW PERSPECTIVE —

How is your head?

Got a thought you can't let go of?
Too many thoughts?
Intrusive thoughts?

How did this happen? It's all their fault.

Gotta buy that new phone—so cool.

They are all idiots. It makes me so angry.

I'm out of here!

This promotion, [job, new career] will make it all OK.

Why don't they listen to me? I'm right.

I still can't believe we broke up?

They need to break up.

What if it doesn't work out? My life is over.

Obsessing about someone or something?
Anxious about life?
Afraid of the future?
Can't sit still?
Can't focus?
Brain blanks out?

—

Let's take a closer look at our thoughts. Let's put everything on the logical, structured timeline. Past, present, and future.

The past: For some, it's great times, happy memories, and past glory. For others it's resentment, regret, guilt, shame, or nostalgia for the good old days.

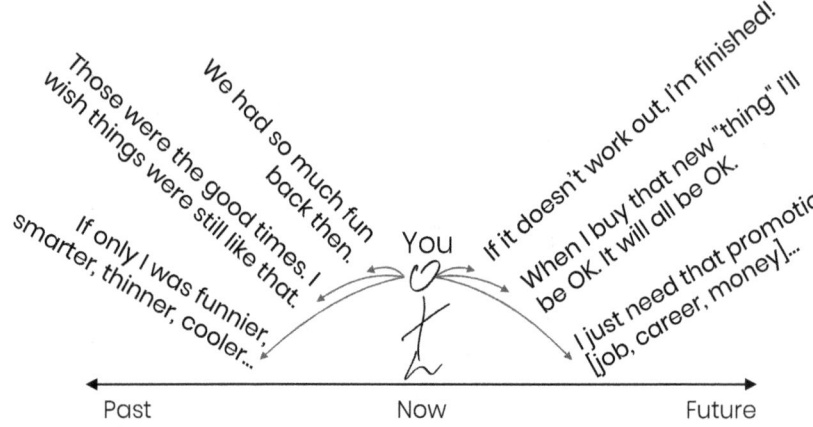

The future: We typically think of this future line as the place to put goals and dreams but it's not. The image above is linear, which can lead to the illusion that we control of all of life, which leads to fear, anxiety, perfectionism, anger, and irrational prejudgement of people, places and things. It is the timeline of the Zero-Sum Game. (Win-Lose.) There is a better option.

— A New Perspective —

Now we can dive a little deeper and look at
one thought that we are experiencing
about the future.

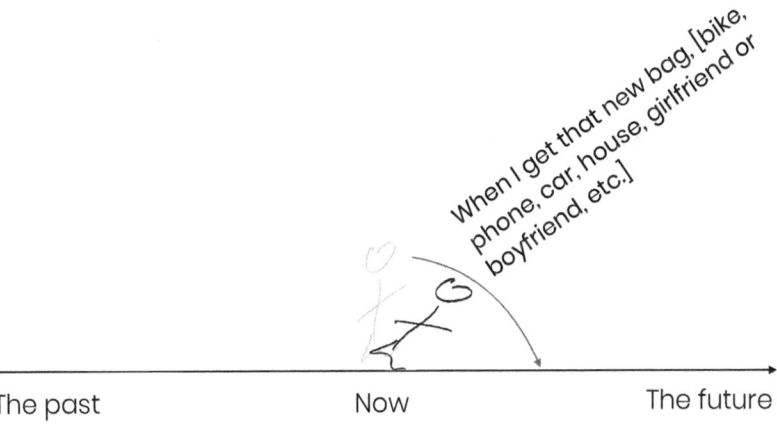

This one thought pulls you out of the present
moment, and it shoots you into the future.

Your attention is split.
More there than here.

You have missed a slice of life.

One thought about the past does a similar thing. It pulls you out of the present and takes you into the past.

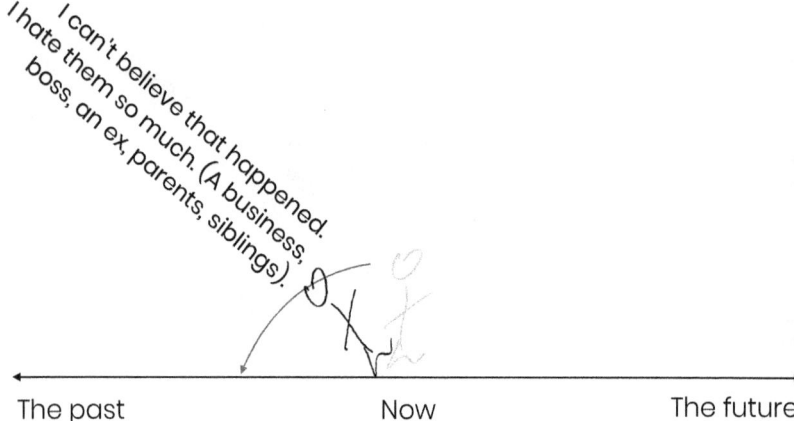

The past — Now — The future

—

Your attention is more there than here.

Life is now, but that one thought of the past took you out of the game.

You have again missed a slice of life.

—

— A New Perspective —

We have thousands of thoughts a day. Some noticed, some unnoticed. Conscious and subconscious. We think to reexamine our past and analyze possible futures on that timeline. Reexamine and analyze. It's very human.

Past Now Future

—

Just because it is human, just because it is common, just because people describe something as natural, doesn't make the thing good for you, or optimal.

These looping thoughts can become a prison.

—

— The Secret Mind of Addiction —

We have multiple thoughts about the past. Individual thoughts, all different, each connected to a different point in time—an event, a situation, or a place.

And we have multiple thoughts of the future. Individual thoughts, all different, each depicting different possibilities and scenarios, connected to points on that future timeline.

You

Past · Now · Future

—

Multiply the number of these thoughts.

See how we miss more little slices of life and spend less time in the present?

—

— A New Perspective —

The more you repeat one thought, any thought, the more anchored it becomes.
It gets hooked into something.

Fixed. Stuck in time.

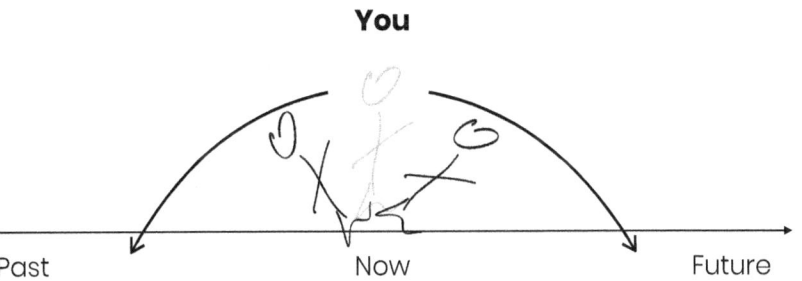

| Past | Now | Future |

—

The more you replay it, the more that thought's pathway gets worn in. It becomes easier to access. Faster to follow. You start to disappear from the present. You lose your presence.

Presence: the state, or fact of existing, or occurring.

This simple act of separation can be enough for us to start numbing and filling that gap in the present with something else such as food, tobacco, or perhaps alcohol or a sugary treat to "take the edge off."

—

Compartments

Your one thought is a pathway through consciousness.

Like a flash, it takes you out of the present and sends you through a wormhole that transports you to a very specific place in your past.

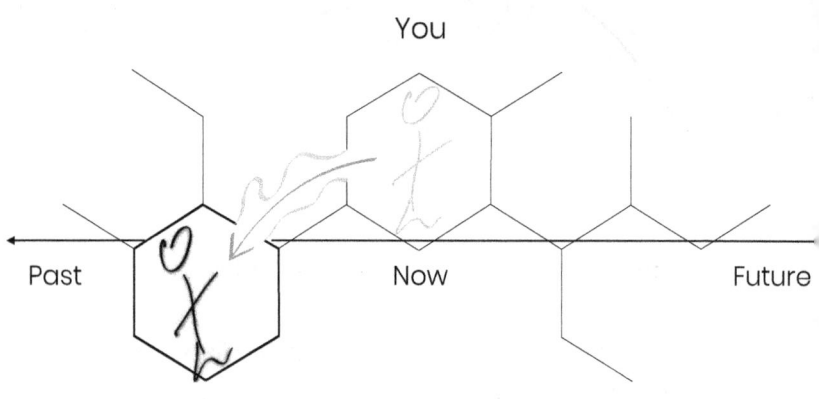

—

Your energy is now diverted there, to the past.

A large part of your presence, your being, is there in the past. A specific spot in time.

It matters.

—

– A New Perspective –

Similarly, obsessive thoughts launch you into the future. Into specific areas of consciousness. Your energy and presence are diverted into specific compartments. Specific situations.

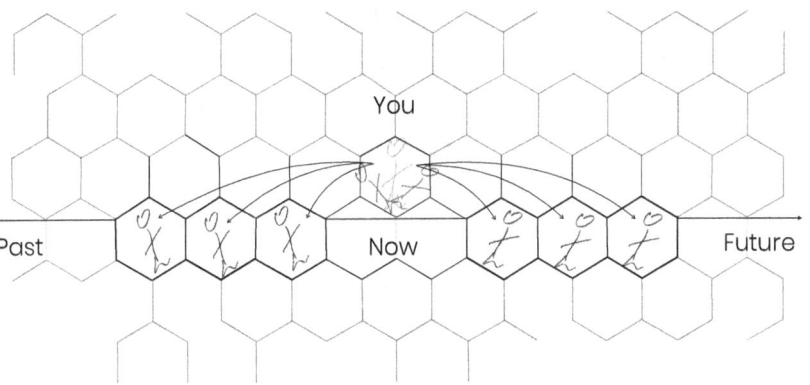

—

People often say they don't feel seen or heard. If your mind is checked out into the past or the thrust into the future, your chance to be seen, to be connected with, to create, and to perform in life has been missed by you. You have taken yourself out of the game.

It's hard to be seen if you are not present.

Your being becomes stretched around the place. Expressions like "bent out of shape" or "not in your right mind" fit the pattern.

The intensity starts to build, so a little more numbing is in order. So we reach for the phone and we scroll or shop.

—

But then you catch yourself, often after you get a nudge from someone or something. Time to "Pull yourself together."

You deploy more energy and more willpower to overcome the thoughts that dragged you into the past and launched into the future.
And you say,
"I'll be OK."

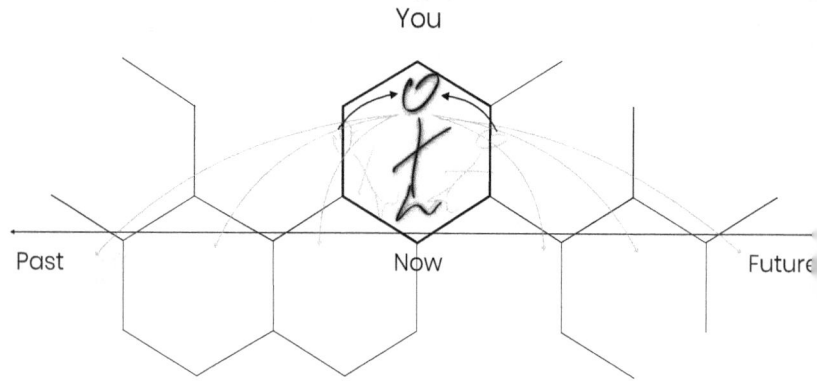

—

And your inner PR department tells the outer world:

"It's OK. I'm OK. I'm good. I'm fine."

Yet there is something that has not been resolved, and so the cycle repeats, and we keep thinking, we keep obsessing, and we keep numbing with substances or acting out.

—

How Addiction Escalates

And life continues... Time rolls on.

Many events in our life go unprocessed; unresolved in our mind. Creating the thoughts we repeat, the thoughts that accumulate over a lifetime.

Things such as family arguments and trauma, lying or cheating, misdeeds and disasters, and everyday life events that we built up in our mind. All these thoughts are hooked in time.

These thoughts are typically accompanied by anger, resentment, and regret for what we did or did not do, and now we have our rationalization to reach for another purchase or prescription to numb that pain.

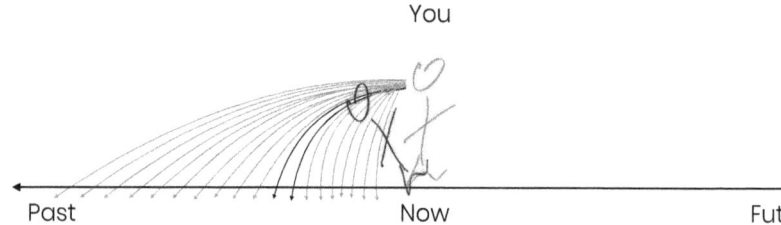

—

Remember… one thought in time
is a channel for energy.
A conduit.

One thought diverts energy down a pathway.

—

– How Addiction Escalates –

The energy flowing to our unresolved thoughts of the past is balanced by energy going into thoughts of the future.

You might have a grand plan, a few audacious goals, and see your empires in the future. Yet this energy is still balanced against the past.

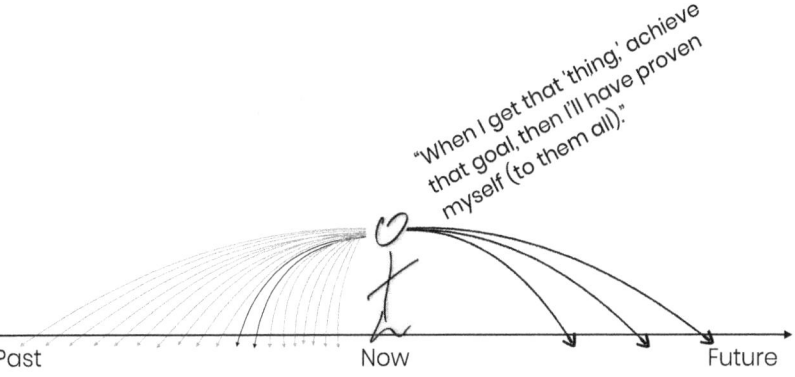

"When I get that 'thing,' achieve that goal, then I'll have proven myself (to them all)."

—

Many goals have been achieved and empires built to prove something. Countless dreams realized to overcome some perceived inadequacy.

The issue with future aspirations is how and why people go about achieving. If your self-worth is pegged to what everyone else thinks of you and you believe that getting the "thing" by itself will fill the hole you feel inside, then eventually, you will end up in more turmoil.

—

If fear and lack kick in, we create a tense attachment to the goal, to the "thing" where we have to imagine every conceivable scenario, and know every possible step, before moving forward, because if we can control every possibility, then we are guaranteed success exactly the way we want it. We will be OK.

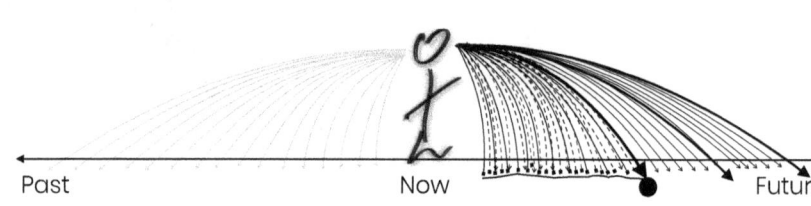

—

The result is overthinking. Analysis paralysis. Stuck in layers of fear and lacking faith. When what we really lack is understanding.

Fear dictates:
"Every step must happen, exactly as you thought it out, to keep you safe and ensure you get that big dream, exactly how you want it. Because then, you will be worthy."

This is life on The Zero-Sum timeline. For anyone to win, someone must lose.

—

How Addiction Escalates

We eventually get going towards our goal, and then we hit bumps along the way, and then we get floored. We are catapulted from an empire in the future, to a negative experience in the past. Filled with negative emotions we collapse. Eventually leaping back to the goal with more effort, discipline, and control. Giving us another reason to drink or numb; the pain of connection we must maintain. It doesn't last...

We bounce around. Past to future. Future to past. Past to future. And we use our addiction to numb us as we go.

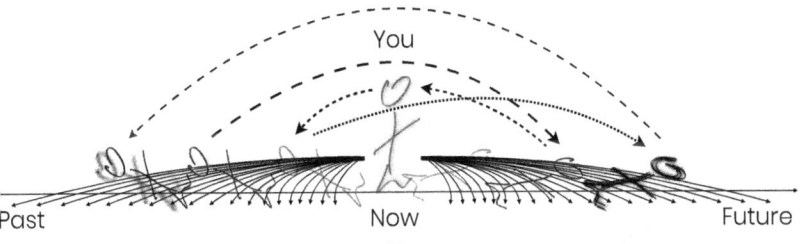

The small positives and negatives we receive from life are amplified and swing us about. Life feels like a washing machine of 'high highs' and 'low lows.'

Confusing. Hard to understand. Hard to escape. Overwhelming at times. You are now a being pulled apart. Not able to do. Not living.

A distorted world view develops, which disconnects us from something, from everything.

And as this disconnection gets worse, so does our coping and compensating to connect. We compulsively control, manipulate, overspend, and overconsume. Food, drugs, plants, alcohol, porn, social media, sex, gambling. We isolate, act out, get angry, induce physical self-harm. And we run. Run from city to city, job to job, or person to person, obsession to obsession.

You

Past   Now   Future

—

Cycles of self-sabotage. Self-defeat.

With the accumulation of obsessive thoughts, the person keeps numbing over things—over everything, (addiction in progression), life takes on a continuous downward spiral.

And in the extreme, a being pulled so far apart, the person's presence in the now, fades completely. They become a shell. A void filled with something unknown.

Living in alternate realities. Out of their "right mind." They disappear. Psychosis. Institutions. Even death.

—

Outside vs. Inside

While the addict, (and friends and family), might see the alcohol, drugs, porn, vapes, pot, sugar, online shopping, debt, doom scrolling, social media, political derangements, vandalism, under earning, and so on, I am highlighting what is happening inside the mind.

The real addiction is inside.

We now go one layer deeper, to get more clues on how to get free.

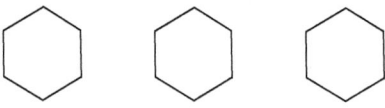

The Clues to Getting Free

> "The truth feels like violence to those addicted to illusion."
>
> Instagram user*

* I cannot find the originator of this quote, so this is best I can do to give them credit. Whoever you are, thank you.

— CLUES TO GETTING FREE —

Why the mental hooks?

Life comes at us. We meet it **how we are**. For example, there is an event, such as a family gathering. Automatically, even subconsciously, we think back to an experience involving our family. A negative one. We are "triggered."

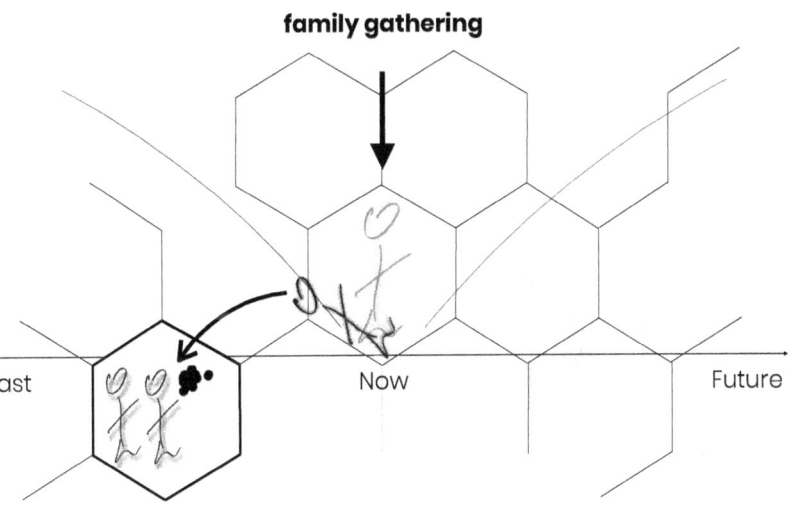

There's a lot of energy around that event for us. It contains something unresolved for us.

In our mind, we spend time in the past event, with the people involved at that time. We relive the experience in that past part of consciousness. Sometimes we add new emotions to it, amplifying it even further.

—

We are then reinfected with the energy of that time. All that energy, all of those feelings and emotions, are brought back into the now, **into your presence**, into this new event.

Hurt, sadness, frustration, self-loathing, or anger from the past come flooding back into us now. Consciously and subconsciously.

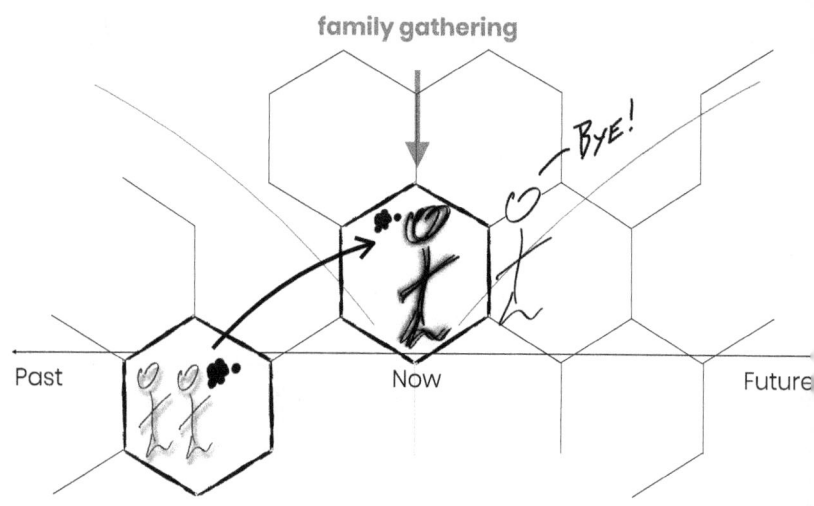

—

Infected with the negative energy of the past, we respond to the current life situation in a disproportionate way. We act out, subdue it, mask it, or numb it with substances. Just one way our visible addictions are triggered.

The next day, we get to add a new item to the list of negative memories we are hooked into.

—

— CLUES TO GETTING FREE —

Through daily life, our minds can spontaneously jump back to a series of wounds and hurts to reference, combine, relive, and reactivate. Splitting us out of the present, and when we want, pulling the negative energy and emotions into the now.

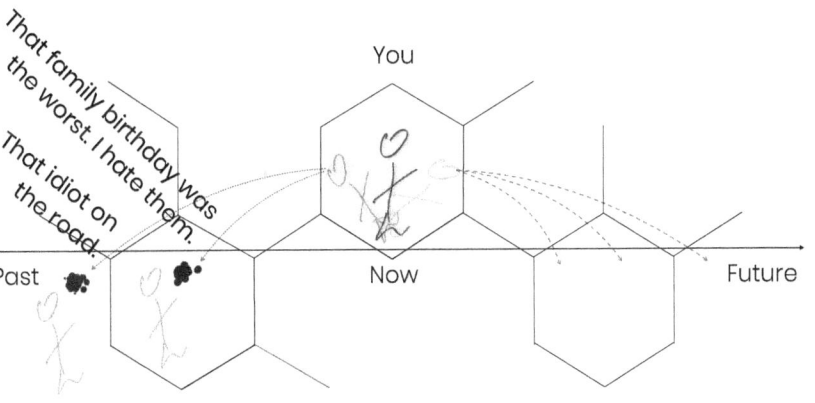

Why are you obsessing about this event from the past? Why can't you just "let it go"?

Are you trying to see something new in that event or situation? Are you trying to figure it out? Is there something you don't want to see? What are you denying?

All of these moments our minds flash back to, are the clues.

Yet life keeps coming at us…

—

Moment to moment, life is constantly changing and moving. Thousands of decisions every day. But with a trail of thoughts hooked into a dark past, life itself becomes a trigger. More events become just like the family event, triggering us to drink, drug, eat, spend, procrastinate, and so on to cope with life. We can no longer respond appropriately.

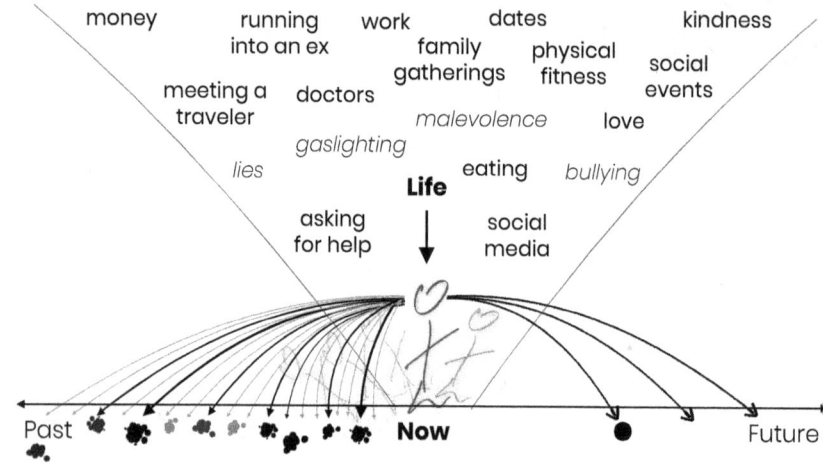

How we respond to life matters. Everything is a communication that sets our future. Not only our actions, but also what we carry in our heart (our beliefs) and in our energy now.

Remember we are exploring the secret mind, the root cause, not just the physical symptoms. Triggers appear to be a cause, however the main clues are the events we flash back to.

― CLUES TO GETTING FREE ―

This mind is set: Stuck living in the past or stuck living in a fixed and fearful future.

Those thoughts, fueling all those feelings and emotions come back to influence you and the world around you, and that present becomes your future.

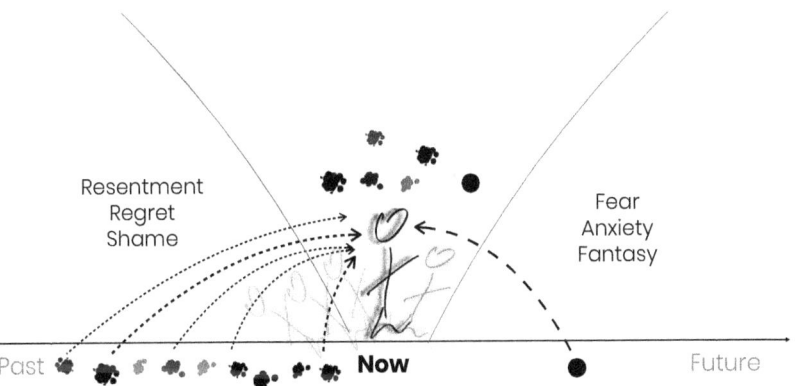

―

With a mind set this way, all manner of symptoms manifest: Overthinking, indecision, procrastination, control, perfectionism, health issues, money issues, and various substance addictions and behaviors to mask, numb, and avoid our responsibility to life.

We are either in avoidance or confusion of how to respond to life. These thoughts are the prison, and living in this state is essentially a death sentence. All that past hurt can kill you.

―

"Let it go" is a trap

We should never even pick up the vast majority of 'things' in life. Yet we choose to pick up certain things and then we can't put them down.

Did "let it go" ever truly work for these bigger issues?

—

Let it go is a trap for most major traumas. It pushes the event away and perpetuates an endless loop of suffering, relief, suffering, relief... Where the addiction is initially the relief and then it becomes more suffering.

"Let it go" denies you a gift—the truth of each situation is the gift that will set you free.

If you resolve these big issues, the mental hooks that pull you apart disappear. There is less of a gap to fill and less pain to numb with our addictions.

—

The Way Forward

Healing the hurt

These hurts—these wounds, traumas, and hauntings from the past—all have hidden gifts. Each hurt can be resolved, and each resolution contains a gift—the truth. A lesson or an insight to give you clarity, and more capacity to live your life forward in gratitude.

As we resolve each hurt, we find mental peace that lasts, and we return to the present. Our presence changes. We are more able to find, and focus on our own gifts, goals, and dreams.

When you learn to resolve one hurt properly, you then know how to resolve them all.

Healing the wounds of the past, does not deny the reality of events, it **transforms** them into assets. We get to know ourselves better. We can find clarity, peace, and purpose from each situation. Resilience, capacity, and capability grow as we do this. We get to like ourselves.

Over time, the popular wellness mantra "I am enough" takes on actual meaning...

I am enough for me.

—

This is not some egotistical claim that we now know all and can sit back, play God, and do nothing. Definitely not. We simply stop going to war with ourselves and with the world.

We find more gratitude for who we are, our blessings, and the gift of this life, and eventually we take the responsibility and the obligation to make the most of our life.

—

Presence needs purpose

To be present without purpose is to be lost and to self-destruct. This is because life is in service to the life around it, and to the greater universe, all arranged to promote more life. To do otherwise is self-destruction. We must have purpose.

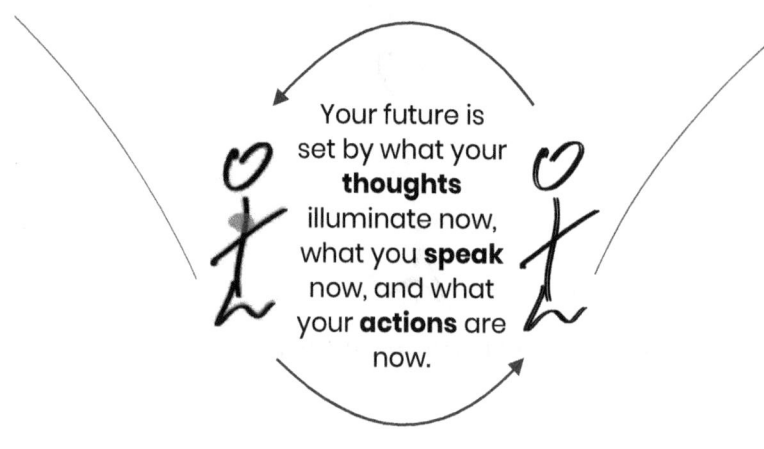

Your future is set by what your **thoughts** illuminate now, what you **speak** now, and what your **actions** are now.

**Being of service.
Being of use.**

—

Yet to be of service to everyone and everything, except ourselves, is to hide. We can become "nice guys" (applying to both to men and women in a pejorative sense), and eventually we get pulled apart and 'dis-integrated,' as illustrated earlier.

—

We must make ourselves useful.

I believe our primary purpose is to serve the world in our own unique way. Making the most of our deepest desires, gifts, or talents. Individuality matters. The highest tier of service encapsulates usefulness to others, to God (Life or the Universe if you prefer), and to ourselves.

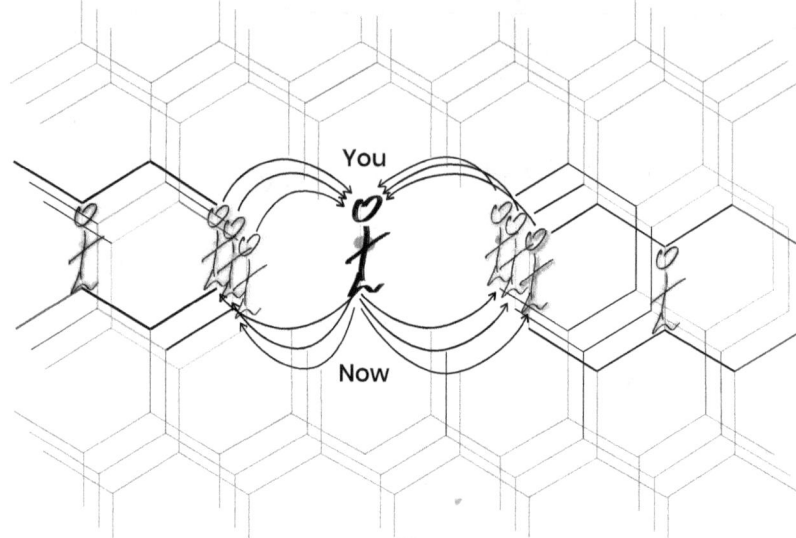

The more you serve in this way, the more you receive. The stronger the cycle grows. Building capacity, skills, connections, and opportunity to deliver more value to more people.

Notice that when we are focused on presence with purpose, we are not pulled into the past or the fearful future. We have been freed from the linear timeline and can now move into the creation plane. The Non-Zero-Sum Game. Here, faith and providence can move mountains.

— The Way Forward —

This is when thoughts, words, and actions are in alignment, and in harmony with the universe. We are in right action toward our dreams. Actual life. Not pulled into the past or fearful future. Nothing to numb, drug, or drink over. You can now live in your very own energetic signature, seen and felt through all of consciousness. You are part of the flow of life.

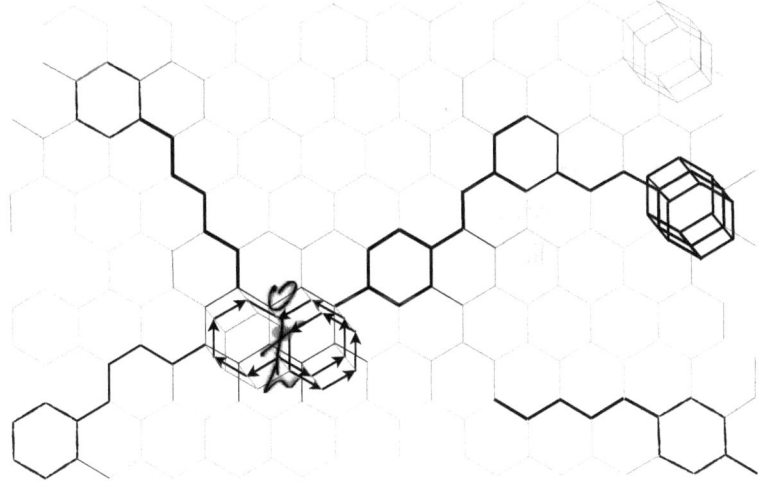

—

You are attracting and creating what is needed—and repelling what is not.

What you seek is seeking you. There are people out there praying for you to appear (be seen), to help them. Just as you have secretly prayed for someone or something to appear and to help you on your journey.

—

> "She's mad,
> but she's magic.
> There's no lie in her fire."
>
> Charles Bukowski

Imagination

A thought can take you anywhere in an instant, but **ideas bring you to life**. They can capture our imagination and energize our whole being. There are no lies in such ideas. We must have an idea of what we want to do, be, or achieve.

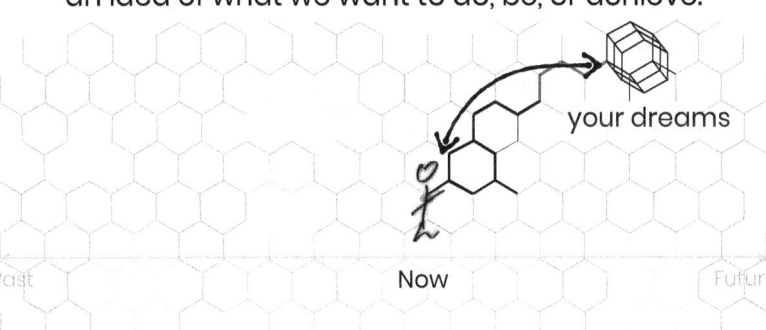

As we transform our hurt, we become more open and awake to the universe, to who we are and what we want. If we get an idea, we have the capacity to do it and to grow doing it.

With a new way of being in the world, we can move toward our dreams without being pulled around on the fear timeline, and without the need for addictions to numb. We realize our dreams on the creative plane.

Some will warn this is ego and that we should listen to God. Maybe that is God, and through right action there is no better way to find out.

Guard your mind

As you transform your hurt, you begin to see other people more fully. You see their 'good,' and their internal divisions, which are mirrored by external decay. Imaginations hijacked. 'Dis-ease' and fear spread from which people need to cope, and by which, they are used for someone else's agenda.

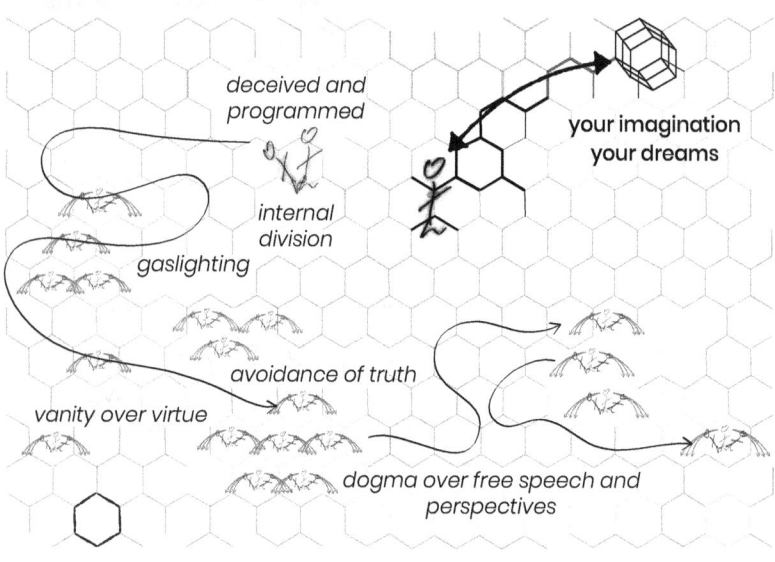

You understand how certain thoughts have become their prison, enslaving them and the world around them. They have become slaves to someone else's purpose.

— The Way Forward —

In a world filled with AI, social media, and mass media calling at you from every turn, the chances of being lied to and gaslit, are greater than ever, causing more distraction, more division in our minds, more hooks we can't let go of, and subsequently more addictions are appearing out in the world.

Your mind and your imagination are one of the most valuable assets you have. They are yours. Guard them. Use them well.

Identifying the hurt

Here is a suggestion to help you identify and resolve each hurt—to find the gift, a truth that will set you free.

Start by focusing on very specific events, and if needed, get right down to the moment a person said or did that one thing that hurt you, which then created the thought that grew in your mind over time.

To help you identify these events, I have listed a range of situations, from general categories down to more specific examples.

My suggestion is to reflect on each category and item below, and see which ones apply to you. Perhaps circle the ones that jump out at you, the ones that you repeatedly think about. Even make a list of events that stick in your mind. Only write down the major events, not every thought.

- family trauma
- business or relationship failure
- bullying (giving or receiving)
- physical events or abuse that left a mental mark
- cowardice and covert agreements
- manipulations including omissions

- outrage at society, politicians, systems
- social media posts and comments
- moments of lying, cheating, stealing
- actions taken to undermine someone
- shame spirals (e.g., you binged on food, drink, or shopping, and then the self-beratement that follows, causes even more harmful reactions by you)
- everyday triggers and flashpoints of anger (e.g., road rage, spilt milk)
- embarrassing flashbacks that reinfect you with shame, guilt, fear, and anger

This exercise of looking in the mirror and getting honest with yourself, can be one of the hardest things you will do, and it is a critical step to getting free. So if you made a list, congratulations, it's a big step forward.

Once you have identified the hurts, pick the ones your mind can't let go of, and search for the deeper truth in each event.

The truth you are looking for is not blaming the other person, place, or thing. This is hard to do when bad things happen to you, but it is a critical principle to follow.

Being alive, inextricably connects us to all of life—we have our part to play in everything.

We cannot control anyone. We can only control ourselves—our thoughts, words, and actions. The truth you are looking for is in relation to you. What is your part? What is it that you don't want to see or accept?

Once you see the truth in each event, you will know it, you will feel it. Even if it's hard to digest—that truth will set you free. It is done. Everything else will flow from that insight. You will have a new understanding of life and a new response to life.

Some people mange to find the truth with specific programs, meditations, journaling, ritual, plants, talk therapy, group meetings, body work, or life coaches.

As mentioned in the introduction, none of those tools worked fully for me, and I found some of them disempowering, which is why I wrote this book, to provide a new perspective on what's really going on in your mind and how that connects to your life.

At the end of this book, I have provided a list of resources from Life Beyond Thinking® that will help you heal fully.

What Helped and Hurt

> "So then, because you are lukewarm, and neither cold nor hot, I will vomit you out of My mouth."
>
> Revelation 3:16
> New King James Bible

What do you want?

In getting sober, as in life, you have to know where you are at and what you want. Outside of peak performers, I see three major clusters:

For some, their life seems good. Family, friends, work, goals, etc., are all OK, but they have an addiction and hurt to address. They should heal those specific wounds and keep all the good stuff. Don't throw the baby out with the bathwater.

Other people need to find truthful goals (ones that they commit to). And with forward-looking, success-oriented friends, their minor addictions will vanish, and their life will change for the better. Keep on that upward trajectory.

Some people are in a nightmare. Hurt, stuck, lost, and addicted, they struggle to know what's what anymore. If that is you, draw a circle around yourself. Now you know where you are. Using the diagrams in this book, you can now identify the hurt. Then find the truth to bring clarity, peace, and purpose.

Get clear on what you want. Decide. Move forward with the right approach, because not everyone needs a radical transformation.

> "Make mistakes of ambition and not mistakes of sloth. Develop the strength to do bold things, not the strength to suffer."
>
> Niccolo Machiavelli,
> The Prince

— WHAT HELPED AND HURT —

Quit your "healing journey"

We do what we value. If you come to value healing, you will keep thinking you are broken and keep looking for wounds to heal. Forever digging in the dirt, forever healing. You'll get good at finding suffering, and you will seek to suffer so that you can heal.

At some point you need to stop this "healing journey" and focus on "living your life" forward. It's probably sooner than you think.

As a suggestion, go back and review the diagrams and the list of addictions and hurts. As you review them, take note (literally write down a list) of the hurts that automatically come up in your mind, the ones that still have a lot of emotion and energy for you. Also note the repeated intrusive thoughts you have, especially ruminating on the past or any fearful thoughts of the future (catastrophizing).

These thoughts—not to be confused with the people or events—are the clues you can use to free yourself for good. Each of these hurts you can transform into a lasting clarity, peace, and purpose.

With this transformation you can command your mind and never be lost in suffering again.

Raise your head and focus on the opportunity of life. The dream. The vision. Yes, there will be challenges along the way, and you will be able to solve them when they arise.

Remember why you started. To simply stop addiction? To get out of mental suffering? To have a better life? To stop self-sabotage and achieve your dream? To feel alive? Resolve the major hurt and keep working toward the dream. Being ambitious and successful is a higher virtue than being comfortable in suffering.

Love and compassion

Love is strict and exact. It is the binding force of the universe. Cycles of life and death, working together, for the overall promotion of life.

Unconditional love is not one set of cosmic rules for one person, and a different set for another. It is the universal laws of life applied **without condition**. It doesn't matter who you are or where you are at, the laws are constant.

If you believe in the Bible, God let his own son (Jesus) die at the hands of a mob. Was that an unloving God that let his son be murdered? Or was there an exact plan of universal law and unconditional love in play, beyond what people could understand at the time? God let his son die, so He could rise to set humanity free for all of time.

Unconditional love can be deployed with kindness and strength, but is equal to all.

Compassion is helping the person learn to help themselves. When we are suffering, that is God's love showing us that we are doing something wrong, that we are missing some part of the map and rules of life. If it keeps repeating (addiction), we end up hurt, stuck, tired and lost. This is still God's love trying to shake us up, to get us up and out of that state.

Expectations are good

People like to say expectations are bad, that they are the mother of all disappointments. And attachment, they say, is the cause of all suffering. Yet, many of those same people "set intentions" and talk of faith, hope, and belief, but many will not mention expectations because they lead to disappointment.

If they have no expectation that their intention, filled with faith, will work, why bother? It makes zero sense. It is time to stop gaslighting yourself into emotional gridlock.

The issue is what you are attaching to the expectation. If you are attaching your entire self-worth to one specific outcome, then yes, that will cause problems. (Note: Self-worth is best fixed by the correct transformation of past hurts. And definitely not by doing esteemable acts.)

Think of it this way. When you throw a steak on the BBQ. Do you expect it to cook? Of course you do, or you would not grill steaks on the BBQ. When you go to work, you have expectations of tasks, purpose, and pay. Your boss and team expect you to do your job (or you won't have one for long).

Setting expectations does not guarantee outcome, or that there will not be curveballs. However, without the expectation of outcome you would not start a task, a project, or anything at all.

I have come to believe that ambition and expectation (knowing) are essential forces of life. They are a mixture of vision, purpose, faith, gratitude, and our will. Each one is specific, and each one matters.

In a world without expectation, nothing would ever happen, nothing would be created, and we would never learn or grow. We'd be sheep scared to dream or to try.

Set expectation of outcome. And if you don't get there, if it doesn't happen, don't wallow in it. Learn exactly why, count your blessings, take nothing for granted, strengthen your faith and purpose, and immediately get moving.

Have ambition, set expectation of outcome, and pay attention to detail. Because your spiritual arrows need to hit their target.

Money

This is a huge topic, and I want to touch on two common and misunderstood beliefs about money that misdirect and stifle us.

One idea that gets promoted, is that "money is evil." Believing this lie will keep you trapped, small, and suffering. Not living your potential. Not serving the world in the unique ways you can. It can even cause people to illogically rage against businesses and systems, and the only thing that happens is that the person who is enraged, becomes trapped by the lie.

What's relevant is the how and why you go about getting and receiving money. Whether it's one dollar or one million dollars, the principles are the same. Let's look at the how and why from two different perspectives.

The first perspective: Are you lying in any way to get money? Do you use inferior materials or ingredients in your products, knowing that it will cause problems and you don't disclose it? Are you knowingly hooking people into repeated patterns that don't serve them? Have you used bribes or insider information to get ahead? Are you looting stores, robbing homes or stealing data? Or do you make money on a popular trend that you know to be a lie?

There are many more examples, and they are all lies of some form, which is stealing. That is evil, not the money itself. **It's us, not the money.**

Now let's look at the alternative perspective: Are you providing services without a word of a lie, and do it to elevate people? To promote more life by coming at life, straight and true, with no lies, manipulations or omissions, and charging full value? Here, money is a measure of what you have already delivered to create more value in someone's life. If you love delivering services and getting paid in this way i.e., making money through right action, is that evil? Or is that a perfectly correct thing to do for yourself, for others, and for society? With right action, you can rightfully receive money. **It's not the money, it's us.** It is our integrity and intention that matters.

The second popular saying is that "The love of money is the root of many evils." This requires context or it can also limit you.

"The love of money is the root of many evils" is really about loving 'things' above all else. Hoarding. Doing anything (lying) to get more. Coveting. Wanting what's not yours. The unearned. It breeds entitlement, a lack of gratitude, and fear. It disconnects you from Life. Once again, **it's us, not the money**.

Suffering is optional

Certain circles tell us that all suffering is necessary, and that life is suffering. I definitely agree suffering is a signal, but saying "Life is suffering," as they trudge around life in self-chosen misery, is vanity over virtue.

If you had a map that shows where humans suffer and where they thrive, then why suffer?

I believe that we stay in extended suffering because of avoidance of our life in front of us, or confusion with life itself. So we drink, drug, eat, numb, or act out in self-defeating patterns, instead of getting honest with ourselves and embracing life head on.

If we personify suffering, here's what Suffering might say. "You can't escape me, I am in charge. You need more wellness, more life hacks, more mantras, more meditation, more meetings. Journal more, ingest more sacred plants, do lengthy morning and evening rituals."

Suffering keeps going. "You can't do that, don't even try. Go on more retreats to calm your mind. Do this cleanse to heal your body. Buy this, buy that. Treat yourself. You deserve it just as you are, because you are worthy right now, no matter what."

And again, and again, Suffering returns to boss us around to enslave us. When we should be seeing it as the signal to stand up and walk free.

We have become slaves to what suffering says. Rather than using our agency to deny suffering its power, we allow it to command our mind and our life. You can take charge. You can address the root cause, and you can keep living life forward, free from prolonged suffering.

If you learn the map and know where suffering is and isn't, you never have to be a slave to suffering again.

FREE: Map of Life

This visual guide shows you where suffering is and isn't. Learn the map, gain clarity, and reduce mental suffering in everyday life.

Get your FREE visual Map of Life here:

LIFEBEYONDTHINKING.COM/MAP

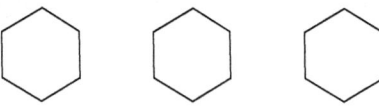

In Conclusion

I wanted to shine a light on the thought patterns that drive addiction, and that the path to freedom, to our quest for life, might just be simpler, easier, and more direct than we keep telling ourselves.

Unfortunately, society programs us with the flavor of the day, filled with confusing and contradictory recovery, wellness and spiritual protocols. Telling us to dumb down, fit in, skip ambition, take it easy; you are worthy as you are, you deserve it; or "service to all" over your prime purpose in life. Follow false gods and gurus, endure endless rituals, take this pill, do that hack, practice fake love and compassion to keep people down and codependent in the very system that claims to get them free.

This book is a call to action for us to take command of our mind and of our life. If you understand the secret mind of addiction, and how it shapes your future, then you can focus on addressing the root cause, find your happiness, and live a vital life forward. And never be a slave to addiction again.

The last page holds one of my favorite quotes which contains an essential truth to personal progress and living fully. Give it a read.

Have fun, and thank you,
Robert De Pinto

– In Conclusion –

FREE Resources

For more insights, tools, and Q&A, please go to the Life Beyond Thinking® community portal here:

LIFEBEYONDTHINKING.COM/FREE

Additional content in the portal includes:

THE STOP DOING LIST. Beyond the addictive act itself, I list multiple things to stop doing now and why.

THE GRATITUDE TRAP. Gratitude is essential to life, and active addicts have very little of it. If misunderstood, it could keep you stuck in a rut. Here I explain aspects of gratitude, why it matters, and tips to find it.

DEFENDING YOURSELF. We have a responsibility to defend ourselves, our values and our sovereignty. I share a simple principle to help guide you in this, and it will help with everyday interactions.

USE YOUR WILL AND YOUR AGENCY. Many people have tremendous will power, and we should not abandon it. I share a very simple technique to let you use it in the right way.

JUDGEMENT AND BEING SEEN. We explore aspects of judgement, and how that fear stops us from being seen, and ways to overcome it.

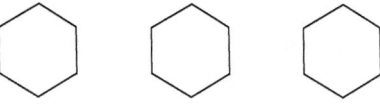

— Author Bio —

Robert De Pinto

Robert has lived a "portfolio life" earning a degree in Mechanical Engineering, became a professional yachtsman, founded multiple technology startups (US Patent), has headed regional corporate roles in Asia Pacific, and lived all around the world.

From the youngest of ages, the world never made sense to him and so a lifelong quest began.

After years of looking—and all the time, money and energy invested in books, coaches, programs and protocols—nothing simply or satisfactorily answered the fundamental questions of what, why, and how… until he discovered a profound map of life, that illuminates how simple it all is.

This map is built on extensive research and practical application. It connects science, philosophy and spirituality, into a unified approach that is simple, visual, and easy to understand.

The secret mind of addiction, is the second book in a series about ending unnecessary suffering and setting humanity free.

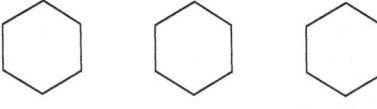

Books and Programs
by Life Beyond Thinking®

A visual guide to spiritual recovery
LIFEBEYONDTHINKING.COM/BOOK1

Home Self-Healing
Heal the hurt for good, and gain a lifetime of mental peace and resilience. This self-guided course does not require any meetings, meditations or guesswork. It is simple, visual, and empowers you for life.
LIFEBEYONDTHINKING.COM/HSH

Addiction Transformation
No meetings. No dumbing down. No guesswork. Transform your addictions for good, and enjoy being you.
LIFEBEYONDTHINKING.COM/TRANSFORM

FREE: The Map of Life
Learn the map, reduce mental suffering and improve flow in your everyday interactions.
LIFEBEYONDTHINKING.COM/MAP

Subscribe
Be informed of new products and events.
LIFEBEYONDTHINKING.COM/SUBSCRIBE

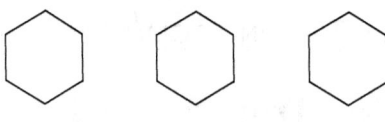

"But when I said that nothing had been done I erred in one important matter. We had definitely committed ourselves and were halfway out of our ruts. We had put down our passage money—booked a sailing to Bombay. This may sound too simple, but is great in consequence. Until one is committed, there is hesitancy, the chance to draw back, always ineffectiveness. Concerning all acts of initiative (and creation), there is one elementary truth the ignorance of which kills countless ideas and splendid plans: that the moment one definitely commits oneself, then providence moves too. A whole stream of events issues from the decision, raising in one's favor all manner of unforeseen incidents, meetings and material assistance, which no man could have dreamt would have come his way. I learned a deep respect for one of Goethe's couplets:

Whatever you can do or dream you can, begin it.
Boldness has genius, power and magic in it!"

W.H. Murray (Scottish explorer and author)
The Scottish Himalaya Expedition.

www.ingramcontent.com/pod-product-compliance
Lightning Source LLC
Chambersburg PA
CBHW060404050426
42449CB00009B/1903